Prison Segmentation For A Prison Game Show

Reverend Mike Wanner

Table of Contents

Introduction

In America alone, there are about 2.3 million people in 6,000+ jails or prisons.

All those prisoners have unique challenges and opportunities which can create challenges to their peace and security. The problems of one prisoner can contribute to situations that could have a domino effect on others under certain circumstances.

I, like most people, was oblivious to that fact until I was invited to look into it. I started channeling Angel Raphael in 2013 and began releasing little message sets as they came through.

In message set 16 of the Angel Raphael Speaks Series there was a message that has remained floating in my head since as a topic for my writing.

"I asked Mike to Step into Prison Energetically

I have asked Mike to get the address and location within a prison of a designated space so he can visit energetically and receive feedback for us. Whether he will have time, interest or opportunity to do this will be interesting to see. As he writes this, he is not thrilled with the idea. We are already consuming a lot of his time."   ARS16

After the First Three Hundred messages, I published Three Angel Raphael Speaks Volumes and much more on healing but the topic of prisons is very complicated, so there was a delay.

Birthplace

I have been blessed to be born in one of the greatest cities of the world, and I now appreciate the gift that was to my life. I invite each of you to look into your own birthplace and see the significance of that to all that comes into your life.

It wasn't until fifty-nine years later that I would find out the significance of Philadelphia to the world. I was graduating from the University of Sedona and visited Spirit Mountain Ranch outside of Flagstaff, Arizona.

Mary Katherine and I were in the yard, and I had just heart-linked with a White Buffalo which went into a stampede and started to roll about in a pile of feed. The buffalo rolled over like a dog scratching its' back.

Mary Katherine looked at me with a twinkle in her eyes, and she said: "Bet you can't do that again." I did, and a different Buffalo rolled in the feed.

From nowhere appeared two women who we had not seen before. When they heard we were from Philadelphia, they were thrilled, and the one said – "Where it all started."

I was shocked by her statement and said - "What Started?" She said "Freedom." The freedom that the world now enjoys started in Philadelphia and I never fully appreciated that.

As we talked, I came to understand that all four of us in the yard that day are Reiki Practitioners and each of us was on our own version of a Spiritual Journey to the ranch. The energy of the place was phenomenal as Native American rituals were frequently practiced there and spiritual power builds over time.

The ladies wanted to stay in touch and promised to send me publications. After returning home, I received the *Sedona Journal of Awakening* in the mail.

The first article I turned to was written by Edna Frankel, an author/friend of mine who lives outside Philadelphia in Blue Bell. The world is smaller than we think and each of us makes a difference.

1 - This Morning

The icing on my prison writing journey came this morning as the picture of a game show came into my mind to answer the question. The question was "How Do I share an awareness of these prison books so that people can get the ideas?"

Prison is not a game and needs to be taken seriously.

BUT

Minds need to open to let ideas in and a way to balance serious matters and process that which one does not wish to hear is to play with possibilities, potentials, invitations, perspectives and ideas from others that you would have never even dream could help.

SO
LET'S
PLAY
Today

2 - I am Writing This Book Because

This book continues to carry the potential for rethinking that can help to reduce incarceration to those who we need to have there.

I want to trigger mindset shifts in the prisoners as well as employees and the community. We need a lot more Objective Productive Dialogues about Enhancing the lives of Prison Employees, Prisoners, Taxpayers and the Families of Each of these groups.

I embraced the Angelic invitation in 2016. So far, The Angel Raphael prodding has had me publish the following books related to prisons:

1. Angel Raphael Speaks Volume 4: Angels, Addicts, Alcoholics & Prisoners - Oh Yeah!
2. Angel Raphael Speaks Volume 5: Prisoners Caring for Alcoholics - Australia In Miniature   Projects Intro
3. Angel Raphael Speaks Volume 6: Prisoners Caring for Addicts - Australia In Miniature For   Addicts
4. Prison Jobs Now: Providing Care For Addicts And Alcoholics
5. Angel Raphael Speaks - Prisons (A Kindle only book -2013)
6. Contained Care Communities: Concept
7. Australia In Miniature
8. Prison Possibilities Dialogue Series: Concept
9. Prison Possibilities Dialogue Series: Volume 2 Dialogues
10. Prison Possibilities Dialogue Series: Volume 3 Dialogues
11. Prison Possibilities Dialogue Series: Volume 4 Dialogues
12. Prison Possibilities Dialogue Series: Volume 5 Dialogues

As I have been writing my books on Prisons, the complexity of the process has amazed me. I have some ideas of ways that might help, but I surrender to guidance.

My guidance suggests that we need a lot of creativity. Open minds on both sides of every issue can make great strides.

My books are about non-confrontational systemic options that could be acceptable options to many residents and management. They are not answers to the specific problems for specific people.

Lawyers are the ones for the job of specific individual help, and a couple of my books invite those professionals to use their skills and creative genius to help get us all out of the taxpayer draining issues of prisons.

The
Intensity
Of
Density
Can
Cause
Enormous
Stress

Segmentation Could Decrease Density And Increase Security

5 - How The Game Show Could Work

The First Priority would be safe for all, and that is why segmentation is part of the setup. While there are many segments to a lot of prisons, the segmentation in my "Prison Segmentation For....." Series is more definitive. I will be offering it free as part of my Christmas 2017 gifting program.

My preferred concept would be to focus on the segmentation programs with efforts that could have a direct link to benefit those that are taking the initiative to help themselves and others Prepare for Successful Re-Entry into the Community at large and or enhance their lives and the lives of their family members in other ways.

There are only ten segmentation books published so far, but there are more in rough cuts of future book projects. The ten books are enough to start as seeds for development.

Let us all begin to play with ideas which could help make this an educational, fun, and transformative experience for Taxpayers, Prison Staff, Prisoners, Prisoner's spouses and families.

It May Be Difficult to See, But Helping Others Can Help Helpers.

The impact of Incarceration involves millions and millions of Americans.

Estimates or Guesstimates for perspective:

2.3 Million Prisoners
2.7 Million Children of Prisoners
2.3 Million Mother's of Prisoners
2.3 Million Father's of Prisoners
2.0 Million Spouses of Prisoners
<u>2.5 Million Siblings of Prisoners</u>

14.1 Million People!

Wow!

14.1 Million People!

7 - What Would Be The Game

The games could take many formats like the game shows on television. I hope that creativity can fill the time with an education that will go deep into the social ills that laid the paths that prisoners followed and the societal enhancements that could fix the potholes in our society that citizens fall in to.

Helping future generations by educating segments of the population in ways to avoid victims would be ideal. Angel Raphael sent a message about that, and I will add it in a later chapter.

I call on prisoners who are able to qualify for a segmentation program in a facility that creates one to develop plans that show potential. Ideally, the show could:

1. Humanize the issues of Spousal Struggle.
2. Humanize the issues of wanting to change without options.
3. Humanize the importance of Childhood Development in a single parent household.
4. Humanize the issues of being suffocated by security without being secure.
5. Identify the importance of capping prison costs.
6. Identify the importance of capping prison occupancy.

7. Identify the importance of prisoner opportunity.
8. Identify the importance of prisoner performance.
9. Identify the importance of a Driver's license for Re-Entry.
10. Identify the importance of Prisoner's family vote.
11. Everything else the prisoners and prisons agree to do.

8 - Benefits All Around

Segmentation in itself will be a benefit to the system and everybody impacted by it along the way. The game show could become famous and bring attention to the under-served.

The success of the show will need to be in segmentation for security reasons for at least a while. Communication with the prisoners from the outside will not be as possible as many would like. That separation for security could provide additional benefit by focusing on benefits to the whole institution and prisoners in general and everybody connected with them all in any way.

Participation would not be a quid pro quo situation but could evolve to benefit particular prisoners by starting a perspective changing situation that will allow many to find opportunities from a softened perspective of the possibilities for prisoners to be rehabilitated.

Consider the value of environmental protection enhancements that benefit the whole community, and you will begin to see how the benefits can go around.

We need to flip the images of everything and allow ingenuity to root and grow an entirely different Group of possibilities for all. Possibilities to include opportunities to showcase:

1. Prisoner Skills
2. Prison rehabilitation successes
3. Correctional Coaching Possibilities
4. Career Upgrades for Staff
5. Educational Enhancements

9 - Help Angel Raphael Be A Prophet

Angel Raphael Clearly discussed the paralysis that so permeates many of the activities of prisons and the possibilities that exist when positive energy is embraced in the thinking of all who live and work in prison. Thought power could be dominant when thinkers set aside personal interest and embrace positive benefits for all. The message as channeled follows.

Prison Life of the Future

The complexity of your prison systems is detrimental to many that occupy, serve, visit, and guard them. There is a palpable intensity of negativity present at most facilities.

When one can change their mind, they can change their reality. Could it be that your society could realign prison life to contain the expansion of the need for more prisons?

Unions should not worry as there is no suggestion that these places can be eliminated any time in upcoming centuries. Union leaders could help serve their members by helping the institutions become more user-friendly and economical for all.

The word economical was included to get the attention of the administrators, but the goal is really to promote the lessening of dehumanization that exists within the societal dynamics from which the crop of criminals grows. The guard and others who work for institutions are exposed to the negative energy of the collected criminals, and that is not exactly a nurturing vibration.

Please consider as if the vibration of a prison existed on a scale that you could read called the love fear continuum. Consider that a single increment move on that scale that went away from fear and moved towards love was actually beneficial to all who passed through the premises.

As you ever so slightly held that thought, you entertained the possibility for a shift for the imprisoned and guards of the future. Congratulations, for you, have allowed some light to shine on a subject that is almost perpetually locked in pessimism. ARS 9

10 - Efficiency Through Positivity

Segmentation and the game show can be the beginning of a positivity shift that starts moving towards higher vibrational living and a de-emphasis on survival struggles. The ability to receive attention and recognition through positive efforts can be transformative over time if the administration and the staff and the residents begin to see the ease in their lives and work together.

Survival skills can be invaluable, but the old adage of "An ounce of prevention is worth a pound of cure" is still valid. Awareness of possibilities and a Pro Bono (For The Good) mindset can allow everybody to step up to a higher level of citizenship.

Segmentation or specific control of spaces can allow possibilities and peace in controlled areas so that struggle and anxiety can fade. As negative energy dissipates, calmness can flow naturally.

Prisons by nature of responsibilities may have a tendency to be cold, institutional and less than user-friendly The subtle goals of segmented areas can continue to focus ideas in positive ways so that community choices can manifest and egos soothed.

If prisoners begin to feel that self-determination is an option, a lot of healing can happen in short order. The rewarding of orderly interactions can be beneficial for administration and the residents.

"What comes around, goes around (Anon.)."

11 - Media Community Effort

Ideally, a community effort could evolve to support the segmentation efforts and especially the game show program. I have already written a book in a copyrighted confidential draft format that I will share with those media agencies that express some interest. The working title, for now, is *Philadelphia Prison Purpose Plan*.

I would encourage a media community effort that involves Public Media, Commercial Media across the whole spectrum of Television, Radio, Newspapers, Magazines, Websites, Social, and Cybermedia carry forth the possibilities and challenges to this effort.

I encourage competition here only to the extent of digging deep into the niches for potential remedies to the problem.

All media is invited to focus differently here than in most investigative reporting. Here please consider yourselves part of a foundation for the optimal method of the future development of an evolving society.

Please keep your investigative blaming efforts separate from this system. We do not need a new fight over what is wrong and who is responsible, we have enough of those battles.

What we need here is the development of what we can do differently in the future so that the problems of now can be avoided.

We need to know what society can do now to get past the problems we have and what we can do in the future to avoid inclining the next generations to prevent those issues.

When I first heard about the program of MADD (Mother's Against Drunk Drivers), I was infuriated. Later, I realized the absolute brilliance of their plan was in keeping others from recreating losses in the future.

Their idea is simple and is akin to closing roads during flood events and snow emergencies. The proactive effort allows the mothers to express themselves in a positive way that will help prevent more damage in the future.

Just like MADD, let us all be about changing the world in proactive efforts that can improve the lives of many people in multiple ways.

12 - Rehabilitation
{From - Prison Segmentation For Safety}

A goal that some folks expect of incarceration is rehabilitation. I hear little about successes in that pursuit but would be delighted to hear of new potentials for that to happen.

I believe that success is more likely if there can be more open-minded, creative thought applied to everything related to prisons and jails and other parts of the legal system.

There seem to be opposing positions on each side of every issue, and I feel that tendency on both the team of administration and the side that is sensitive to the incarcerated. I suggest to both points of view that there is needed a hand to all things that minimize opposition and promote team efforts to finesse new ideas that benefit all the interested parties which would include the Prisons, the Prisoners and especially the taxpayers.

All three interests are diminished by opposition by anybody to anything. Interestingly, I see higher value in saying and doing nothing than there is in opposing anything suggested by anybody.

Fractional progress can be much more efficient than absolute objection. If all parties agree on the part of an idea, then we have real growth.

With any luck in prison, Congress may adopt the process and America can thrive. Prisons and Prisoners and taxpayers can lead the way. My question is - Will You? Will We? Will They?

13 - "The Pope Went To Prison"

{From - *Prison Possibilities Corrections Coaches: Concept* }

"While that sounds like a joke setup, it is the truth. Pope Francis visited the Curran-Fromhold Correctional Facility which is about twenty minutes from my house.

The Pope's visit to Philadelphia and the World Meeting of Families on September 22-27, 2015 was quite a remarkable event in Philadelphia. The tour was well covered by the media as it highlighted inclusiveness.

I hope you can use that visit as inspiration to be inclusive also. You are in the position to accelerate inclusiveness by balancing potential and possibility.

Time Magazine has a transcript of his remarks according to the Vatican Press Office. See the whole talk at http://time.com.

I listened to the entire speech attentively, and the part that moved me was:

'This time in your life can only have one purpose: to give you a hand in getting back on the right road, to give you a hand to help you rejoin society. All of us are part of that effort, all of us are invited to encourage, help and enable your rehabilitation.

A rehabilitation which everyone seeks and desires: inmates and their families, correctional authorities, social and educational programs. A rehabilitation which benefits and elevates the morale of the entire community.

Jesus invites us to share in his lot, his way of living and acting. He teaches us to see the world through his eyes. Eyes which are not scandalized by the dust picked up along the way, but want to cleanse, heal and restore. He asks us to create new opportunities: for inmates, for their families, for correctional authorities, and for society as a whole.

I encourage you to have this attitude with one another and with all those who in any way are part of this institution. May you make possible new opportunities, new journeys, new paths.

All of us have something we need to be cleansed of, or purified from. May the knowledge of that fact inspire us to live in solidarity, to support one another and seek the best for others.

Let us look to Jesus, who washes our feet. He is 'the way, and the truth, and the life.' He comes to save us from the lie that says no one can change. He helps us to journey along the paths of life and fulfillment. May the power of his love and his resurrection always be a path leading you to new life."

Thank You
Pope Francis

14 - Universal Prayer For Prisons
{From - *Prison Possibilities Corrections Coaches: Concept* }

Prayer Suggestion For Prisoners, Prison Staffers, Public Officials, Medical Practitioners, and Correction Officers/Coaches

God Almighty

I/We recognize you as the source of all good, all healing, all wholeness, all wellness and all support for your offspring in all matters.

I/We unify with your Divine Will and strive to respect all your children in all situations with the same dignity and respect that you do. We appreciate your helpful direction, guidance, and protection as we go out to interact with all your children in the world.

I/We claim our highest skilled functional awareness under your direction and our ability to hear the things to do and the words to say. I/We claim all the healing needed for all of us is now optimized as this claim is declared. As we invite all this or better now, I/we also ask for you to have us do nothing if that is the best of all.

I/We accept that the optimized situation for all is started, increased and fulfilled now.

My/our sincere Thanks to you Dear God, AND SO IT IS!

15 - Wrap Up

I would encourage every prison authority and administration to consider segmentation and the game show concept. Please read the following first.

Disclaimer

I, the author, am not involved with prisons or prisoners but I have talked to many prisoners during Hospital Pastoral Visitations. I am sharing what is coming to me in an effort to spread understanding and trigger conversation that can be helpful. It may be that the discussion needs finessing and I invite your wisdom into the mix.

My guidance has suggested that a lot can be done. I will detail my views which are not the expert positions of a Corrections Officer or Corrections Administrator or Corrections Manager or Corrections Supervisor, or Medical Practitioner or Psychologist or Psychiatrist or Social Worker or another expert who might be helpful here.

As I have said many times before, everything that I look at about prisons seems to be so complicated. Here I have suggested some things that have come to my awareness.

Please feel free to discuss these ideas in your community.

God Bless The United States Of America!
AND SO IT IS!

16 - A Potential Program

Philadelphia has played a big part in the history of everything in America. That Famous Liberty Bell rang so loud that it cracked.

A former jail and present tourist attraction is called Eastern State Penitentiary, and it played a role in the early days of incarceration, and the type of imprisonment called solitary confinement.

I wrote a book about solitary called *Solitary Community* because the old ideas have deep roots. I believe that efficiency and ancient ideas are not compatible in the troubling financial times in which we live.

America is struggling financially because we are not very progressive with the human dignity that we offer offenders. We can improve on our decency as a nation, and I recommend that we do.

Prison Segmentation and a Prison Game Show can help us get a handle on our problems and use the money of American Taxpayers in a way that is more humane to offenders and taxpayers alike. I hope Philadelphia and your city try these out.

Reminder

Please remember what Pope Francis said in a Philadelphia Prison in 2015 - "Let us look to Jesus, who washes our feet. He is 'the way, and the truth, and the life.' He comes to save us from the lie that says no one can change."

For
Considering
These
Ideas

Ever

It Does Not Help Prayer Still Does!

Resource: http://www.Create-A-Prayer.com

19 - Resource Books

Distant Healing Sessions (or Join Mail List) – Write To mikewann@voicenet.com

Books by Rev. Mike at www.Amazon.com

Veterans Healing Six Pack
1. *Trauma Healing Options for VA Hospitals: Help for Veterans to Own Their Healing and their future.*
2. *Trauma Healing Action Steps for Veterans: Help to Start Healing*
3. *Trauma Healing Action Steps for Veterans: Empowerment*
4. *Trauma Healing Action Steps for Veterans: Forgiveness*
5. *Trauma Healing Action Steps for Veterans: Thought Freedom*
6. *Tea For Veterans: Welcome One Home*

PTSD Power Pack:
1. *The PTSD Project: Turn Pain To Power*
2. *PTSD & Soul Retrieval: Putting One Back Together*
3. *PTSD & The Purple PAD: Calling all Scientists and PTSD Patients*

Angel Raphael Speaks Volume 1: Take Courage! God Has Healing in Store for You!
Angel Raphael Speaks Volume 2: Take Courage! God Has Healing in Store for You!
Angel Raphael Speaks Volume 3: Take Courage! God Has Healing in Store for You!
Angel Raphael Speaks Volume 4: Angels, Addicts, Alcoholics & Prisoners – Oh Yeah!
Angel Raphael Speaks Volume 5: Prisoners Caring for Alcoholics - Australia In Miniature Projects Intro
Angel Raphael Speaks Volume 6: Prisoners Caring for Addicts - Australia In Miniature For Addicts
Reiki Journaling from Japan
Reiki Is Alive: God's Great Gift
Four Parts to Healing
Distant Healing: We Are All Connected
Stress Release Energy Work: How To Cope
Does Reiki Love Heal Cancer?
Group Consciousness
Salute To Philadelphia VA Medical Center: Thank You
Reiki Transcript for Reiki 2 & 3 Channels: Dr. Usui Is That You?
God Bless Kindle & Amazon
Puppies Are Different From People
If Your Dog Dies
Toy Guns Are Obsolete
Great Spirit Made Children With Red Skin: AND
The Cage of Fear: Is Not Locked
God Made Children Red, Yellow, Brown, Black & White: Greet Each Child...

Emergency Medical Kindness In The Cradle Of Liberty: Big City - Cracked Bell
Angels Are Always Around Addicts and Addicts: Help Is Near Now! Invite It In!
Angels Are Always Around Addicts and Alcoholics: Volume 2 - Tools To Help Re-Light...
Prison Jobs Now: Providing Care For Addicts And Addicts
Controlled Care Communities Concept
Prison Possibilities Dialogue Series: Concept
Prison Possibilities Dialogue Series: Volume 2, 3, 4, 5 Dialogues
Prison Possibilities Voluntary Exile
Prison Possibilities Corrections Coaches
Prison Possibilities For Mexicans: Is A Boat Better Than A Wall?
Prison Possibilities Family Time: A Reason to Thrive!
Prison Genius Pool: "So Much Genius In Jail."
Prison Possibilities Access Control: Prisoner Access by Request
Prisoner's Lawyers Can Save The American Economy: Make A Buck Doing It & ...
Prisoner Family Talks, Days, Stays & Vacations: Connecting Helps Healing
Prisoner Writing Projects: Write To Heal, Start Over & Reconnect
Prison Cell Clearing & Blessing: Clear Entities, Chase Ghosts, & Create Sacred Space
Prisoner Professors: Show You Are Aware Create Change With Care
Prison Reiki? Maybe Someday? A Gateway To Help Heal Prisons & America?
Judges and An Angel Rule On Possibilities: We Can Cut Sentences & Prison Costs
Ideas For Prison Wardens: Leadership Is Not Easy
Solitary Community: Could Community Support Cut Costs and Issues?
Prison Project Communications Team: Communications Can Change Lives
Motivating & Empowering Prisoners? Invite Prisoners To Find Their Motivation
Prison Segmentation For Safety, And Sanity, Security, Peace, and Space
Prison Segmentation For Security
Dowsing for Prisoners; Answers from Above
Ex-Prisoner Possibilities With Real Estate Investors
Prison Segmentation For Joint Ventures
Prison Segmentation For Your Rehabilitation: R U Ready?
Prison Segmentation For Family Villages
Prison Segmentation For Senior Prisoners
Prison Segmentation For Coaching Clubs
Prison Segmentation For Miracles

Little Books on Kindle.com by Rev. Mike:

English Medical History Questionnaire For Non-English Speakers
English Language Helper For Non-English Speakers
Wise Wonderful Women Are The Well Of The Family
Answers for Test & Research: Dowsing Power
Crisis? Reiki! Baby? Reiki!
Bible References For Healing
Angel Raphael Speaks – Prisons
Angel Raphael Speaks – Veterans
The Saint Off Interstate 95

20 - Angels Please Prayers

Addict's

Angels of Healing Selected
Help Me to Stay Directed
Come To Me From The Sky
I Am Ready to Succeed Not Try
If I Don't Invite You In
I Might Not Win
I Have Been Lost For Too Long
Help Me To Stay Strong

Alcoholic's

Angels of Healing On High
Help Me to Stay Dry
Come To Me From The Sky
I Am Ready to Succeed Not Try
If I Don't Invite You In
I Might Not Win
I Have Been Lost For Too Long
Help Me To Stay Strong

From

http://AngelRaphaelSpeaks.com/AAAAAAA/

21 - Private Channeling

Angel Raphael Speaks a series of free messages that are channeled through Reverend Mike Wanner for the Highest good and Highest Healing of all concerned.

Many questions arise about Reverend Mike doing private channeling, and he does help with that so e-mail him.

Reverend Mike is available worldwide as a psychic channel, emotional release facilitator, spiritual energy practitioner & teacher, and public speaker. He looks forward to meeting you soon!

Email - mikewann@voicenet.com 215-342-1270 PRIVATE SPIRITUAL READINGS/channelings or Spiritual Healing Sessions: Telephone or in person. Rev. Mike is available for private, one-on-one intuitive sessions with you, his Guide Family, and your Guides.

He helps by offering clarity on emotional situations about your life, your purpose, your spirituality, and the release of stuffed emotions and cellular memory.

Connect to the love of your Guides today!

Contact Rev. Mike for an appointment.

Sessions available:

Spiritual Readings
Angel Channeling
Distant Reiki Healing
Remote Clearing of Stuffed Emotions
Distant Clearing Cellular Memory
Distant Clearing Energy Blockages
Remote Clearing of the Chakras
Customized needs
Mastermind dowsing responses to yes/no direction finding questions.

Rev. Mike is a facilitator of healing. He brings you and the Divine together so that you can align with the Divine and have a great time and a great life. All healing is between you and God, as it should be.

Go ahead and start without Rev. Mike. Visit his prayer site http://www.Create-A-Prayer.com. Take the first step NOW.

22 - Reverend Mike Wanner

Rev. Mike Wanner started his Metaphysical and Ministerial studies with Reiki in 1993 and had studied seven styles of Reiki in the U.S., Japan, Canada, Denmark and Australia. He is certified to teach. He became certified to teach Integrated Energy Therapy in 1999 and co-taught the first IET class of the new Millennium. Mike began dowsing in 2001.

Ordained as a Metaphysical Minister of the International Metaphysical Ministry and an Interfaith Minister of the Circle of Miracles Ministry, Rev. Mike practices and teaches spiritual energy therapies in the Philadelphia Area.

Rev. Mike holds ministerial degrees from the University of Metaphysics and the University of Sedona. He is a Pastoral Care Associate at Aria - Frankford Hospital. He taught at the National Academy of Massage Therapy and Health Sciences.

Rev. Mike was a faculty member of the Medical Mission Sister's Center for Human Integration's School of Integrated Body/Mind Therapies in Fox Chase, Philadelphia, PA for twelve years.

Rev. Mike is licensed by the teaching of Intuitional Metaphysics to practice Spiritual Healing and Scientific Prayer. Mike is also a Prayer therapist.

Rev. Mike was elected in 2007 to the status of "Fellow of the American Institute of Stress."

In 2008, Rev. Mike became a practitioner of Coincidental Recognition as he incorporated the CoRe System into his spiritual healing practice.

In 2009, Rev. Mike trademarked a new healing process called Quantum Quatro! Subtle Energy System Support®.

In 2011, Rev. Mike joined the outreach program known as the Health Advantage Group.

In 2012, Rev. Mike became a Certified Professional Coach by The Master Coaching Academy and Joined the Personal Empowerment Group.

Before his Metaphysical, Ministerial and Coaching studies, Rev. Mike worked for Sears Roebuck and Co. while in High School and after graduation, until he joined the U. S. Air Force in 1965. He returned to Sears from Vietnam in 1969 and stayed until 1978. His final Sears assignment was as an efficiency expert in Methods - Operational Research and Development.

He volunteered with Burholme Emergency Medical Services from 1969 and is still a Life Member and Board of Directors Member. He started a private ambulance company in 1975 and worked professionally in the field until 2001 when he devoted his full attention to real estate investing, healing, coaching, and writing.

□

May All Who Read This Be Blessed
AND SO IT IS!